NORTH ANTRIM

Volume One

A COLLECTION OF PHOTOGRAPHS

By

Arthur Ward

This publication was kindly sponsored by

Footwear BISHOPS Limited
Established in 1840

Dixons
OF COLERAINE

Radisson

RADISSON ROE PARK
HOTEL AND GOLF RESORT

ROSSWILSONARTIST.COM

LYNAS
FROZEN FOODS

Published by Arthur Ward

Photographs copyright
Arthur Ward 1997

Design & Layout
Arthur Ward

British Cataloguing in publication Data:

Ward, Arthur - North Antrim, Vol.1.

ISBN: 0-9533577-0-8

Printing, binding and colour reproduction by The Universities Press (Belfast) Ltd.

The author wishes to thank the sponsors of this publication.

Cover Photograph: Kenbane Castle

Sea mist - Knocksoghey and Sheep Island

INTRODUCTION

This book has evolved out of a passion for photography which I have pursued for many years, combined with a love for the natural environment of North Antrim. I was fortunate enough as a child and later as a teenager, to spend many idyllic years with my grandparents in the townlands of Craiganee and Cloughcorr near Ballycastle. During summer months I would spend most of my time exploring the 'nooks' and 'crannies' of my surroundings with numerous camping expeditions to Knocklayd, Murlough Bay, Kenbane Castle, Dunluce Castle and the Giants Causeway.

On occasions I would stay with an uncle in the village of Ballintoy who kept a small fishing boat at the harbour. It was from here that I enjoyed fishing trips off the coast, dulse gathering on Sheep Island and pleasure trips to Portrush, Ballycastle and Rathlin Island. One of his many interests was beachcombing and often after a storm I would accompany him on walks along the cliffs, descending to the many boulder strewn bays in search of bounty washed ashore by the North Atlantic. The experiences of this part of my life have left me with a deep affinity for the area, especially the coast, which never ceases to inspire me.

Photography has always been a creative pastime for me. I do not claim to be a professional in any way, nor do I claim that any of these photographs are superlative. They are simply the results of one man's pastime, like many others my photographs are as much the results of luck, persistence and weather watching as they are of any technical experience.

With this book I have set out to create a collection of photographs that, in my opinion, encapsulates the beauty and essence of North Antrim and I hope the scenes within will serve as a small momento of this natural splendour. I have tried to keep the text to a minimum, leaving the photographs to speak for themselves. To keep the collection manageable, I have divided it into two volumes - this volume covers from Curran Strand at Portrush to Fair Head near Ballycastle while volume two will cover Rathlin Island and the Glens of Antrim, along with many other inland locations.

For the technically minded, all the photographs were taken with a standard 35mm camera and two lenses, a 28-70mm and a 70-300mm lens. I complete my equipment with a sturdy tripod, a lightmeter, polariser and a couple of graduated filters. Film stock used was Fuji Velvia 50 and Kodak 64 & 25 colour reversal film.

Arthur Ward

Late autumn - Curran Strand, Portrush

At anchor off the Skerries - Portrush

Curran Strand - Portrush

Stretching from Curran Strand to Dunluce Castle are the limestone cliffs of the White Rocks. These soft sedimentary rocks have been carved through the centuries into a labyrinth of caves and arches, they are interspersed with the distinguishable shapes of Shelagh's Head, the Giant's Head, the Wishing Arch and the Lion's Paw. The limestone cliffs end suddenly against a dark basalt outcrop majestically crowned by Dunluce Castle and joined to the mainland by an arched walkway - underneath lies the Mermaid's Cave which is accessible from the land or sea.

Built by Richard de Burgh during the Anglo-Norman period, the Castle has seen many additions to its structure over the centuries. It gradually fell into disuse during the mid 1600's when the last occupier, the Earl of Antrim, moved to Glenarm Castle. Excavations of a souterrain inside the walls produced evidence which indicates the site was in use from the sixth century.

A short walk away from the castle lies the old church and graveyard of St. Cuthbert's, dedicated to a Northumbrian monk and dated to the 1630's. Originally thatched, the church was built on the site of an older building and was in use up until the 1820s when the new church of St. John's was built in Bushmills nearby.

Local folklore tells of Spanish Armada sailors from the ill-fated 'Girona' being buried here in 1588 but the earliest identifiable stone dates to 1630, ten years after the Pilgrim Fathers landed in New England.

Winter -The White Rocks

Late evening light - The Giant's Head

Sunset - Dunluce Castle

Dunluce Castle

St.Cuthbert's Church

At the mouth of a shallow valley - once the outflow of melting glaciers - is the small fishing village of Portballintrae. The harbour itself is protected from the open sea within a small horseshoe bay.

This picturesque location has sweeping views of the Causeway headland and becomes a hive of activity during the summer months but as autumn approaches, the village slowly returns to its much treasured peace and tranquillity. It is one of the best winter locations to view the swell of a North Atlantic gale as it surges into Portballintrae Bay.

One mile upstream is the small town of Bushmills. Formerly known as Portcaman, the town developed with the rise of water powered industries during the 1600's. Although primarily famous for its whiskey production, it was also the site of the first hydro-electric tramway in the world.

Above the town the river Bush drops twenty or so feet over the Walkmill falls and into a shallow gorge. It then flows over several weirs through the town before meandering out over the flood plain and into the North Atlantic at Portballintrae. The falls, known locally as the 'Salmon Leap' provide an ideal spot to watch these ocean travellers as they negotiate the final barrier on their long journey home to the spawning ground.

Portballintrae Harbour

Leslie's Pier - Portballintrae

Salmon Cottage - Portballintrae

Salmon fishing - Bushmills

The Mill - Bushmills

The Walkmill Falls - Bushmills

Cross in St. John's - Bushmills

Old farm buildings - Tonduff

The coastal scenery adjacent to the Giant's Causeway is some of the most beautiful and awe-inspiring that you are likely to find anywhere in the world. It encapsulates a beauty and wildness that can touch a deeper part of the human being, whether you visit during the tranquillity of a summer's day or in the face of a howling winter gale you will not leave unmoved by the landscape. The majestic cliffs and inaccessible bays combine with myths and legends to inspire but look carefully and you will see in the landscape traces of another reality - isolated ruins, kelp walls and shoreline fields - testament to a harder life of subsistence farming and fishing endured by past generations on this wild and untamed coastline.

Many ships have foundered along these shores, but none so tragic as the 'Girona', a galleass of the Spanish Armada. Carrying many Spanish noblemen and the crews from two other Armada shipwrecks, the 'Girona' was on passage from Killybegs to the relative safety of Scotland. As she rounded Inishowen peninsula, heavily overladen and in deteriorating sea conditions, her rudder failed. In the teeth of a north-westerly gale, the crew fought for hours to keep her off the coast but she finally struck Lacada Point, near the Giants Causeway at midnight on October 30th. 1588 with the loss of over twelve hundred men. Only five are believed to have survived.

The Grand Causeway

Treading the Causeway Stones

Plaiskin Head

View to Lacada Point and Spaniard Rock

Past Bengore Head to Ballintoy and Fair Head

Horseshoe Harbour - Port na Plaiskin

Port na Truin - Benbane Head

Port na Brock, Portfad and Contham Head

Portmoon Bay to Dunseverick, Ballintoy and Knocksoghey

Dunseverick and Knocklayd mountain

Salmon Cottage - Portmoon

Dunseverick Castle stands on a basalt outcrop surrounded on three sides by the sea. Part of a tower is all that remains of the castle which was destroyed by a Scottish army during the rebellion of 1641. Dunseverick is known to be one of the ancient sites of Ireland - references to it in the Annals of Ulster put its founding date as 1525 BC. One of the great royal roads from Tara - seat of the kings of Ireland - ended here and many heroes of Irish myths and legends such as Cuchulain, Queen Maeve and Turlough are closely associated with the area.

It is known that Saint Patrick visited Dunseverick on several occasions and christened people here - one of whom later became Saint Olcan, Bishop of Armoy. Anyone who walks up to the castle and takes in the view of Portmoon can rest safe in the knowledge that they have walked in the footsteps of Saint Patrick. A well which exists a few feet from the cliff edge is named after him and is reputed to be one of the holy wells of Ireland.

A short distance away is the small fishing harbour of Dunseverick. Uninhabited and sheltered amongst basalt islands, it is a haven for summer picnics and winter storm watching. Many people began their long emigration trail from here, being rowed out to catch a passing schooner bound for Glasgow or Derry where they would embark on one of the many emigrant ships to Australia, New Zealand or the Americas.

Dunseverick Castle from Feigh mountain

Portmoon from Dunseverick Castle

Atlantic swell - Dunseverick Harbour

Dunseverick Harbour

Sunset - Dunseverick Harbour

One hundred feet above the sea and in view of Benbane Head and Scotland, lie the ruins of Templastragh. It contains the remains of one seventeenth century church and two graveyards - one Irish and one Scottish. The church was built on the site of an older building believed to have been founded in 648AD.

Just around the corner is the secluded salmon fishing hamlet of Portbraddon which looks out across White Park Bay to the basalt islands sheltering Ballintoy harbour. The sand-dune area behind the bay was one of the first settlements of Neolithic man in Ireland. Evidence of these early settlers remain in the hearths and flint implements which are exposed in the dunes by winter winds and by the passage tombs which stand on three surrounding hills.

The picturesque tower of Ballintoy Church looks deceptively Mediterranean. In fact, it once supported a steeple which was removed by a hurricane in December 1894 - leaving it with its present unique character.

A narrow winding road takes you from the church down to the fishing harbour of Ballintoy which looks out to Sheep Island and Rathlin. The small limestone harbour is synonymous with the fishing and boat building traditions of the North Coast. It was used extensively during the late nineteenth century to ship local sett stones from Brockie Quarry, where over one hundred men were once employed shaping the sett stones which went to pave the streets of Dublin, Cork, Wexford, Limerick and Glasgow.

Templastragh Church

Storm Clouds - White Park Bay

Passage Tomb - Ballintoy

Early morning - White Park Bay and Portbraddon

Evening light - White Park Bay

Ballintoy Harbour and Sheep Island

Ballintoy Harbour

Sunrise - Bull Point, Rathlin Island

Ballintoy Church

Evening rain showers - Ballintoy Church

Spanning a chasm some eighty feet deep is the famous Carrick-a-Rede Rope Bridge. Although a working bridge for the salmon fishermen, it is today widely used by the passing visitor. The island has a small salmon cottage which has access down steep steps to a boat quay from where the nets are tended.

A few miles along the coast is the secluded remains of Kenbane Castle. Exceptional in its location, the castle is built on a limestone headland which rises from below the surrounding basalt cliffs. It was built in the mid 16th century by Colla MacDonnell, brother of James and Sorley Boy of Dunluce - it is believed the castle was occupied right up until the 18th century.

Between the limestone headland and the shore is a small cliff known locally as 'The Old Man of Kenbane' - when viewed from afar - it resembles an old man with a staff climbing up from the sea with the majestic headland of Fair Head rising behind.

Fair Head rises six hundred feet above sea level and has spectacular views of Rathlin Island, Murlough Bay and the Mull of Kintyre in Scotland. Travelling inland brings you to the village of Armoy, situated on the river Bush and location for the only round tower in North Antrim - dated to the 9th century. Close by is the enchanting tree lined road of Bregagh.

Evening shadows - Carrick-a-Rede Island

Carrick-a-Rede Rope Bridge

Sea mist - Carrick-a-Rede

Rain showers - Coolmaghra and Fair Head

Kenbane Head and Rathlin Island

Salmon Cottage - Kenbane

Kenbane Castle

Gathering clouds - Fair Head

Round Tower and St. Patricks Church - Armoy

Bregagh Road - Armoy

Fair Head and Altnacarry Head - Rathlin Island